£1

The Road to Resurrection

Cowley Publications is a ministry of the Society of Saint John the Evangelist, a religious community of men in the Episcopal Church. Emerging from the Society's tradition of prayer, theological reflection, and diversity of mission, the press is centered in the rich heritage of the Anglican Communion.

Cowley Publications seeks to provide books, audio cassettes, CDs, and other resources for the ongoing theological exploration and spiritual development of the Episcopal Church and others in the body of Christ. To this end, it is dedicated to developing a new generation of theological writers, encouraging them to produce timely, creative, and stimulating publications of excellence, and making these publications available widely, reaching both clergy and lay persons.

The Road to Resurrection

Meditations on Walking the Way of the Cross

G. Corwin Stoppel

Cowley Publications
Cambridge, Massachusetts

Published in the United States of America by Cowley Publications, a division of the Society of Saint John the Evangelist.

Library of Congress Cataloging-in-Publication Data:
Stoppel, Gerald C., 1952-
The road to Resurrection : meditations on walking the way of the Cross / G. Corwin Stoppel.
p. cm.
ISBN 1-56101-212-2 (pbk. : alk. paper)
1. Stations of the Cross. I. Title.
BX5947 .S8S76 2003
232.96—dc21

2002155702

Cover and interior art: Sharyn Laughton, Art Offerings
Cover Design: Kevin R. Hackett, SSJE and Jennifer Hopcroft

This book was printed by Transcontinental Printing in Canada on acid-free paper.

Cowley Publications
907 Massachusetts Avenue
Cambridge, Massachusetts 02139
800-225-1534 • www.cowley.org

To my beloved wife, Pat Dewey

I am deeply indebted to Theodore Kimball, Fred Leslie, and the members of the Knights Templar who made possible my pilgrimage to Israel in February 2000; also to Ezra Eini, our incredible guide throughout our visit to his country. Above all, I wish to thank my wife Pat Dewey, our parish secretary Thomas Vandenberg, and all the friends and members of All Saints' Episcopal Church in Saugatuck, Michigan, who encouraged—and sometimes kept after me!—to complete this book.

Contents

Preface

A Pilgrimage through Jerusalem

In recent years the ancient practice of pilgrimage, making a journey to a holy site for spiritual benefit, has enjoyed an astonishing revival. One thinks immediately of holy places like the Isle of Iona in Scotland, the Holy Isle of Lindesfarne and the Shrine of Our Lady of Walsingham in England, Santiago de Compastela in Spain, the Taizé Community in France, and, of course, the Holy Land itself. But in many ways, the destination is incidental to making a pilgrimage. It is the act of going, doing, *walking*—and returning home—that matters.

I invite you to join me on a very particular path of pilgrimage through the streets of Jerusalem, down the *Via Dolorosa,* the Way of the Cross, tracing the path that Jesus took as he walked to his crucifixion. Along the way, we'll make several stops—fourteen in all—and consider the events that took place there nearly two thousand years ago. At each station (a word that means *stopping place)*, we'll pause for a moment, as long as necessary, to pray and reflect on our own way of suffering, remembering that Jesus has not only gone this way before us, but indeed, is with us on the way now.

Perhaps you have been to Jerusalem and know these sites well. But even if you have not, I have endeavoured to describe each station in such as way as to give you a verbal glimpse of its spiritual shape and significance. Each chapter of this book is preceded by an evocative piece of original art by Sharyn Laughton; you may find these intentionally abstract images helpful in focusing your prayer as you read. In any case, my prayer is that your faith will deepen as we walk the road to resurrection together, as we encounter the Lord on the way, and that you will "return home" more healed, whole, and filled with the resurrection life.

Introduction

Setting the Stage: Palm Sunday to Maundy Thursday

In order to walk the Way of the Cross, we do well to remember what happened immediately before Jesus' original trek along this road on that first Good Friday. We need to spend some time looking at three events that took place earlier in that week and the politically charged context in which they occurred.

Palm Sunday: a threat to the established order

The books of Matthew, Mark, and Luke—often referred to as the Synoptic gospels because their common subject matter and similar phrasing suggest a literary interdependence—all report that Jesus and his disciples arrived in Bethany (also known as Bethphage), directly across the Kidron Valley from Jerusalem on the Mount of Olives. They came there by way of

Jericho, the home of Nicodemus, one of Jesus' secret disciples. This is important to note, for it was Nicodemus, along with Joseph of Arimathea, who took charge of the burial arrangements following Jesus' crucifixion and who brought a large supply of spices to prepare his body. Although we have no indication that Nicodemus and Joseph had ever met, Nicodemus may have been fully apprised of Jesus' plans and aware of what might befall him in Jerusalem.

All three gospels report that by this time the Temple authorities were already plotting to capture Jesus quietly and kill him without creating a public uproar. But all three accounts provide few details about what Jesus did once he and the disciples arrived in Bethphage; instead, they continue with their story of Jesus' instructions to go into Jerusalem to find a particular donkey that he could ride into the Holy City.

The twelfth chapter of St. John's gospel records a similar story but with additional important details. Six days before Passover, John tells us, Jesus and his disciples arrived in Bethphage, where they stayed in the home of his longtime friends Mary, Martha, and Lazarus. We are also told that this is the same Lazarus whom Jesus had raised from the dead. The raising of Lazarus had created such a stir in and around Jerusalem that it was soon brought to the attention of the Temple authorities, who were appalled not so much at what Jesus had done as by the way that this miracle had enhanced his reputation and drawn an even larger crowd of followers to him. Their jealous anger was so great that, according to John 11:54, it was no longer safe for Jesus to be seen in public. The chief priests issued an order that news of Jesus being found anywhere in Israel was to be reported to them so that he could be arrested. The implication in John's gospel is clear: after the notoriety caused by the raising of Lazarus, Jesus and the disciples had withdrawn from Jerusalem and Bethphage, returning a week or so later, just in time for Passover.

Once back in Bethphage, Jesus and his disciples celebrated the Sabbath together with their friends. Jesus made no attempt to disguise or hide himself; as a result, word of his presence spread quickly throughout the community and into Jerusalem. Although Jewish law limited the distance anyone could travel on the Sabbath, before long, a large crowd had gathered outside Jesus' friends' house.

This was most alarming news to the Temple authorities and other religious conservatives, if for no other reason than that it was so close to Passover. Jerusalem was already crowded with tens of thousands of Jews from all across Israel and much of the Roman Empire, and more were arriving daily. Among them were many who had come from Galilee. This region, where Jesus had spent most of his ministry and where he had a large following, was a province known for its political unrest. Given the often inadequate logistics of feeding, housing, and providing even minimum sanitation for so many people, Jerusalem's resources were stretched beyond capacity. With so many people crowded together, tensions were running high. The additional problems Jesus' presence in the city would cause were the last thing the Temple leadership needed. The gospels tell us that the Sanhedrin (the Jewish High Council) met in special session to seek a way to rid themselves of both Lazarus and Jesus.

There were several reasons why they would want to kill both of them. First, the Sanhedrin wished to do away with Lazarus because he was the recipient of the great miracle recently performed by Jesus. It was one thing for a miracle to have occurred in Galilee or another outlying region of the country—stories could be more easily denied or controlled. But as long as Lazarus was alive and living so close to Jerusalem, he functioned as living evidence of the spiritual power and authority of Jesus. The Sanhedrin believed that if they could kill Lazarus, then perhaps they could convince the people that Jesus had not raised him from the dead, but only temporarily cured him of some illness. In time, the story of his "resurrection" would be all but forgotten.

Additionally, many of the more conservative members of the Sanhedrin believed that Jesus was usurping too much of their authority over the people. Their anxiety was more than mere jealousy. In an age in which most people believed that anything extraordinary was a miracle or sign of divine intervention, Jesus' power and the people's belief in him seemed boundless. The Temple authorities had good reason to worry that more and more people might turn to a popular religious figure such as Jesus. Unless he was stopped, he would continue to undermine their power base.

At the same time, the Temple authorities feared that Jesus might *not* be able to continue performing miracles or that in time the people would come to expect more than he could deliver. For decades, there had been itinerant preachers, healers, and assorted miracle workers traveling throughout the country. Some of them were genuine, albeit limited in their powers; others were charlatans. Sooner or later they had all disappointed the crowds, and the people turned against them, feeling cheated, used, and disillusioned. Each time this happened, there was the risk of increased secularization—more people turning away from the true worship of the Lord God. In other words, the Council believed that eliminating Jesus would prevent the erosion of the Jewish faith.

Many of the more conservative Jews, especially the Pharisees, believed that Jesus was a liberal blasphemer who did not obey either the regulations concerning behaviour and ritual observance that they were developing at the time or the laws of Moses. They could cite numerous examples, some of which are recorded in the gospels: performing miracles and healing people on the Sabbath, eating without first ritually washing his hands, forgiving the sins of others, and referring to himself as the Son of God and the Son of Man. Jesus was known to associate with prostitutes, tax collectors, religious zealots, foreigners, the mentally ill, and others beyond the pale of acceptable society. Above all, he refused to accept into his group any disciple of another teacher, and he seemed to acknowledge no accountability to anyone other than himself and what he claimed to be his instructions from God.

The Pharisees were waging an intense battle against the

secularization of their age. Even though the Romans granted almost unprecedented freedom of religion to all its subjects, they built shrines, temples, and altars to their own gods wherever they went. The ruins of such sites can still be found throughout Europe, the Near and Middle East, and North Africa. For the most part, these shrines dedicated to Roman gods created few problems for the indigenous people—like the Romans, most of them were polytheists. The Jews, however, were strict monotheists; to them, the very presence of pagan temples in their land was anathema.

Recent trends alarmed the Pharisees even more. After the elevation of Julius Caesar to divine status following his assassination in 44 BCE, the Romans had begun worshipping their emperors as living gods. Many among the conquered peoples throughout the empire, especially those who aspired to a better life, sought to accommodate their overlords by worshipping the Roman deities. The result, even in Israel, was syncretism—religious practice that blended elements from different traditions. It was this trend that the Pharisees abhorred most. They believed that Jesus' flouting of the Mosaic law was exacerbating this trend, undermining their attempt to restore the purity of the Jewish religion.

Despite the growing dangers associated with returning to the Jerusalem, Jesus chose to make a bold and dramatic entrance into the Holy City, all but guaranteeing that everyone would learn of his presence. This story is so well known to Christians that its oddities and complexities are often missed. Only by examining the events of Palm Sunday in detail can we understand the message Jesus was trying to convey.

The entrance into Jerusalem is the only occasion on which the four gospels or any of the noncanonical books note that Jesus rode on an animal. We read that he walked from his home in Nazareth to the Jordan River to be baptized. During his forty-day sojourn in the rugged Judean wilderness, he was on foot. Throughout all of his ministry, Jesus and his disciples walked from one village or city to another, traveling at least once, if not several times, from Galilee to Jerusalem and back—a distance of well over one hundred miles. What, then, is the significance of the fact that on Palm Sunday he chose to ride from Bethphage into Jerusalem, a distance of less than a mile?

Another peculiarity adds to the intrigue: all three Synoptic gospels record that Jesus instructed two of his disciples to go to a specific place in Jerusalem, borrow a donkey

(Matthew, quoting Zech. 9:9, mentions a donkey *and* its colt) that they would find there, and bring the animal back to Bethphage so he could ride back into Jerusalem. If Jesus' feet had been sore or injured, he could have easily borrowed a mount in Bethphage; no doubt many of his followers gathered there would have been delighted to lead him into the city on their animal and then ride it back home. Why would Jesus have gone to the trouble of borrowing an animal in Jerusalem unless there were other issues at stake? Moreover, consider the instructions themselves. If the owner asked why his animal was being taken them away, Jesus told his disciples to answer, "The Lord needs them."

It is highly doubtful that any owner would have found such a response sufficient to allow two strangers to walk off with his livestock. The only plausible explanation is that all of this had been prearranged by Jesus or by one of his friends, perhaps when he was last in Bethphage a week or so earlier. But this explanation only raises additional questions: Who was the owner of the donkey and its colt? Was telling the owner, "The Lord has need of it," a simple way to let a friend know that Jesus was back in the area—or was another, more important message being communicated?

Although the biblical record is silent on these matters, Jesus' conscious choice of a donkey indicates that he went to such lengths in order to make a symbolic statement, one based on ancient traditions of the Middle East. When a king entered a city, he didn't walk—that was something commoners would do. He rode, either in a chariot driven by one of his servants or on an animal. Riding in a chariot symbolized that the king was entering the city as a conqueror. If he rode on a horse, that told the inhabitants that he was coming to make war on them. But if he rode into a city on a lowly donkey, that was meant to assure the people that he was coming in peace. So by riding into Jerusalem on a donkey, Jesus was announcing to friend and foe alike that he was a king coming in peace.

John 12:15 records the moment as a fulfillment of an ancient prophecy foretelling the coming of the King of Peace, which said, "Do not be afraid, daughter of Zion. Look, your king is coming, sitting on a donkey's colt!" Indeed, all the gospel accounts describe the people's joyous greeting of Jesus as a reception befitting a king. Some onlookers climbed into the palm trees along the road. Others broke off palm branches to wave. Still others lay the branches or the cloaks from their backs onto the ground before Jesus, shouting, "Hosanna!

Blessed is the one who comes in the name of the Lord, the King of Israel!"

To be sure, Jesus' teachings, the miracles he had performed, and his ability to befuddle the Pharisees in open debate all contributed to the crowd's enthusiastic welcome. But there was more: people believed him to be a direct descendent of the great King David. The significance of a royal lineage is easily lost on many modern Christians. At the time, however, many saw Jesus as the rightful heir to the throne currently occupied by Herod.

But in evoking his lineage through the symbolic gestures he made in his entry into Jerusalem, Jesus gave more credence to an already lengthy list of accusations his opponents would soon make against him. One of the charges the chief priests laid before Pilate was that Jesus was a rebel and insurrectionist. After all, he had spoken of a kingdom. Many people had already begun to proclaim him as their king and Messiah. What better time to start an uprising than the beginning of Passover, when there were huge crowds in Jerusalem, full of religious fervor and passion? Shouldn't the emperor's representative in Palestine be troubled by such a possibility?

No status quo: a challenge to the Temple's leadership

After arriving in Jerusalem, Jesus spent the next few days in the vicinity of the Temple, most likely returning to Bethphage each night. While he was in the city, he spoke openly, taught many of the parables recorded in the gospels, healed the sick—the same activities that made him a troublemaker in the eyes of the religious and secular authorities made him a beloved leader in the eyes of the people. Many eagerly awaited the moment that he would proclaim himself king and lead a revolt against Rome. He refused to do this, but instead made use of an incident at the Temple to articulate the nature of his kingship.

The four gospels describe in varying ways how Jesus took a length of rope, fashioned it into a whip, and then, in a fit of civil disobedience, drove the merchants and money-changers out of the Temple. Like his entry into Jerusalem, this event warrants closer scrutiny.

The Temple was constructed like a series of nested boxes. At the very center was the holy of holies, the sanctuary in which the Ark of the Covenant was kept. It was there, the Jews believed, that God resided when visiting the earth. This area was so sacred that it was off limits to everyone except the chief priest—and even he was allowed to enter it only on the eve of Passover, at the conclusion of all the other rituals, to make his sacrifice on behalf of all the people of Israel. Jewish men worshipped in the part of the Temple that lay just outside the holy of holies; beyond that was an area reserved for Jewish women. Still further out, on the porches built by King Herod the Great, was an area open to all.

This outer plaza was near the wide gate where worshippers exited the Temple; there people could wait for those who were still inside. The area had become a meeting place where friends and strangers might gather to talk, where informal religious debates were held, and where men argued nuances of the Law. Most important, it was the one place that Gentiles—anyone who wasn't Jewish—could come to find out more about Judaism and the God of Israel.

At Passover, Jerusalem was extremely crowded with worshippers who had come to make their annual sacrifice at the Temple. For those living in the city or the immediate vicinity, this presented little challenge. From their own herds they could select the required yearling lamb and take it to the Temple. But for those who came from the outlying regions or other countries, the annual sacrifice required careful planning. For their convenience, shepherds had set up stalls on the outer plaza where the out-of-town worshippers could buy the animal they needed for their sacrifice and Passover meal.

Similarly, the Temple authorities had allowed moneychangers to set up stalls on the outer plaza for the sake of convenience. Since the Mosaic law forbade the making of graven images or likenesses of any living thing—human or animal—people wishing to make a monetary contribution to the Temple treasury could not make their donation in Roman coin. After the Romans conquered Palestine in 63 BCE, they imposed their coinage, which bore the likeness of the ruler. To intentionally place one of these coins in the Temple coffers was blasphemy—and it became even more of a blasphemy after the Roman Senate proclaimed Julius Caesar a god. The moneychangers, after weighing and measuring the Roman and all other foreign coins, would convert them into the Jewish coins that were acceptable for making donations to the Temple.

The moneychangers' and herders' commercial activity on the outer porch of the Temple was at its height during Passover. That is, at the very time that Gentiles would be most likely to want to congregate on the porch to learn about Judaism, it was unavailable to them. Foreigners thus had no place where they could ask the priests and rabbis questions about the worship of the God of Abraham, Isaac, and Jacob. Moreover, many of the merchants charged exorbitant prices for their animals and many of the moneychangers were less than scrupulously honest in their dealings because they knew their patrons had no other recourse. And to make matters worse, the Temple authorities allowed this to happen because they received a portion of the profits.

According to Mark 11:17, Jesus chased the merchants and moneychangers off the outer plaza, saying, "Is it not written, 'my house shall be called a house of prayer for all nations'? But you have made it a den of robbers." In effect, this action accused the religious leadership of subverting the fundamental purpose of the Temple by permitting it to become more of a marketplace than a place for people who wanted to worship and learn about God. Though the religious authorities accused Jesus of adulterating Judaism, here Jesus was calling their own purity into question, setting his leadership and vision of faithfulness in sharp contrast with their own—but also creating additional problems for himself when they took him before Pilate.

Fit for a King: a symbolic location for a symbolic meal

The third major event that merits close inspection occurred on what Anglicans now call Maundy Thursday (the name derives from the Latin, *mandatum*, meaning, "commandment," and refers to the new commandment that Jesus gave his disciples after he washed their feet, John 13:1-11). Jesus dispatched Peter and John to make arrangements for their Passover meal. A casual reading of the twenty-second chapter of St. Luke's gospel gives the impression that this was done at almost the last possible minute—almost as an afterthought—but that is unlikely for several reasons. For one, Jesus had announced his intention to go to Jerusalem to celebrate Passover weeks earlier. Moreover, Jerusalem was bursting at the seams with people; it would have been nearly impossible to find a sufficiently large room to accommodate Jesus and all the disciples, had he waited until the very day of the feast to look for a place. The disciples also recognized the problem, for they asked him, "Where will you have us prepare it?" almost as if they were sarcastically asking, "And just where in the world do you think, at this late date, we're going to find a place? You should have thought of this before now!"

Upon closer examination, Jesus' instructions to the disciples make clear that this was not a last-minute arrangement, but rather something that, perhaps like the donkey for his ride into Jerusalem, had been carefully orchestrated well in advance. The disciples were to go into the city, find a man carrying a water jar, follow him back to his home, and then tell him, "The teacher says to you, 'Where is the guest room where I am to eat the Passover with my disciples?'" The householder would then take them to an upper room that had been reserved for Jesus.

Readers of the Passion narrative who have never been to Jerusalem (and even those who have) often miss the Upper Room's highly symbolic location: according to tradition, it was directly over the Cenacle, that is, the tomb of King David. The actual location of David's tomb had been long forgotten, but sometime after the return of the Jews from their Babylonian Captivity an arbitrary decision was made to build a shrine for him on Mount Zion in Jerusalem, and it has remained a sacred site to this day. Centuries after the shrine to David was built, a Christian chapel was constructed directly above the Cenacle, and the legend developed that this was the place where Jesus and the disciples celebrated the Last Supper. This chapel was later destroyed, then rebuilt in the twelfth century by the Crusaders. Thus, visitors are not seeing either the actual Upper Room or the exact burial spot of King David.

But here the symbolism is far more important than historical accuracy. By placing the two shrines together, the gospel account once again underscores the Church's teaching that Jesus was a direct descendent of the great king, a true member of the house of David.

As we make our way through the Stations of the Cross, we now have a better appreciation for why Jesus was so despised by the Temple authorities: he had symbolically proclaimed himself to be the Messiah; he had challenged their authority over the affairs of the Temple; and he was asserting his royal lineage. Taken together, these actions led the Temple authorities to view Jesus as a dangerous threat—but they profoundly misunderstood his mission. The gospel accounts of several pivotal events in days leading up to Good Friday—Jesus' entry into Jerusalem, his encounter with the moneychangers and merchants at the Temple, and the Last Supper—skilfully suggest that the kingship Jesus proclaimed was of a fundamentally different order than the one for which many people were hoping. Jesus wasn't trying to liberate the Jewish people from Roman authority; he was trying to liberate people's hearts and minds from spiritual bondage, from an attachment to anything—money, power, fame, security, affection—that separated them from God.

The First Station

Jesus is Condemned to Death

The first nine Stations of the Cross are located on the streets of Jerusalem's Old City, beginning at the Antonia Fortress and ending at the entrance to the Church of the Holy Sepulchre. The tenth through fourteenth stations are within the ancient church itself.

According to tradition, the *Via Dolorosa* begins at the remains of the Antonia Fortress, a massive stone structure built by King Herod the Great (appointed King of the Jews by Rome in 40 BCE, and ruling until his death in 4 BCE, this Herod was the one associated with the Massacre of the Innocents) in honor of his friend and political mentor, Marc Anthony. The fortress's four immense stone towers still stand, a symbol of the power Rome exerted over this region from 63 BCE to 66 CE, and then again without interruption from 135 CE until the Persian invasion in 614 CE. Today, all that remains of the original building inside the fortress can be found on the campus of El Omareigh College and within the Chapel of the Flagellation and the Church of the Condemnation. (Inside the latter is a magnificent mosaic depicting Pilate symbolically washing his hands of guilt after condemning Jesus to death.)

One of the building's unique features is the *Ecce Homo* (literally, "behold the man") archway over the street. For many years, pilgrims walking the *Via Dolorosa* were told this was part of the original Antonia Fortress, and the very place where Jesus was presented to the crowd after he had been sentenced to death. More recent research has concluded that this archway was built much later, most likely after 135 CE, by the Emperor Hadrian in commemoration of his triumph over the Jews in the Second Jewish Revolt.

Within the original fortress were numerous state rooms, offices, private chambers, and apartments for the Roman administrators; the Praetorium, or Court of Law; and the barracks for the Roman soldiers stationed in the city. Although Rome maintained tight control over its provinces, for the most part the Roman governors attempted to curry the favor of their subjects by working with, not against, local political and religious leaders. In all likelihood, therefore, with Passover at hand, most of the Roman soldiers stationed in the city would have been confined to their barracks within the fortress to minimize the chances of antagonizing the Jews in their religious observance. That said, the soldiers would have been prepared to rush to any trouble spot within a matter of minutes.

Then, just as today, a soldier's life was an endless stretch of tedious routine work punctuated by moments of great tension and anxiety. With time weighing heavily on their hands, no doubt many soldiers found diversion in gambling. Carved into a slab of rough pavement (the *Lithostrotos*) in the outer courtyard of the fortress is a game of chance known as the King's Game, somewhat akin to a miniature version of hopscotch. Using dice carved from wood or bone and reeds to move their markers from one spot on the board to the next, the soldiers would make wagers on the throw of the dice. Sometimes the stakes were the clothes and possessions of criminals condemned to death.

It was to this site, perhaps just a few minutes after sunrise and most certainly before the streets were too crowded, that Jesus was brought on this Day of Preparation for Passover, having spent the previous night in the dungeon at the chief priest Caiaphas's palace. The trip would have taken less than half an hour. Jesus' guards would have bound his hands in front of him, using the long end of the rope as a leash to lead him. Additional guards in front and back would have been present to make sure he did not escape or that his friends could not rescue him. Members of the Sanhedrin would have accompanied the procession to present their complaints before Pilate.

According to John 18:28, the Temple authorities would not defile themselves by entering the fortress—doing so would have made them ritually unclean just before the holiest day of the year. Biblical and noncanonical accounts state that Pilate came out of his apartment to meet with the delegation on the pavement in front of the Antonia Fortress. Were special pleas or negotiations necessary in order to persuade Pilate to do this? The gospels are silent on the matter, and there are no Roman records of this initial encounter; however, a noncanonical book, *The Acts of Pilate* (also known as *The Gospel of Nicodemus*), describes in great detail the events that took place when the Temple authorities brought Jesus before Pilate.

According to this text, Jesus was accused of being an ordinary man with no theological training who had blasphemously described himself as the Messiah and the Son of God. He was also charged with being a violator of the Sabbath, a miracle worker whose power could only have come from Satan, and a sorcerer. The laws of Moses demanded the death sentence for even one of these charges, the Temple authorities argued.

But the Jewish leaders did not have the right to impose and carry out an order of execution—only the Romans could do that. Intrigued by the Sanhedrin's charges; Pilate ordered one of his aides to spread a small cloth on the ground for Jesus to walk on. When the Temple authorities objected, Pilate mockingly retorted that he himself had seen other Jews bowing down to acknowledge Jesus as a great spiritual leader. He had heard how others had spread their garments and palm branches before Jesus earlier in the week—so he was only granting Jesus the same courtesy that his own people had extended.

Pilate then summoned Jesus to accompany him into the fortress for a private interview. As Jesus passed by, the busts of the Roman gods bowed down before him. When they heard of the strange miracle, the Temple authorities protested that it must have been a trick. Pilate repeated the test, this time ordering some of his men to bring the busts out to the street so that the accusers could see it for themselves. Just as before, when Jesus passed by, the busts bowed down before him.

The Acts of Pilate also records (as do the gospels) the story of Pilate's wife sending a message to him, warning him to have nothing to do with such a good and just man as Jesus. Pilate wanted to defer to the wishes of his wife, but the Temple authorities persisted in their accusations, this time adding that Jesus was allegedly born out of wedlock, that he consorted with Greeks and other Gentiles—some of whom were also suspected of being born out of wedlock—and that he had violated numerous other Jewish laws. Pilate, however, remained unimpressed with these seemingly minor charges.

At this point, according to *The Acts of Pilate*, Nicodemus, a member of the Sanhedrin, spoke on behalf of Jesus, telling Pilate of his good works, and arguing that Jesus had done nothing to deserve the death penalty. Immediately after Nicodemus finished, several people who had been healed by Jesus came forward to tell of what he had done on their behalf. At this point, other Temple authorities and members of the Sanhedrin accused Nicodemus of being prejudiced because he was a secret disciple of Jesus.

Although lacking many of the details mentioned in *The Acts of Pilate*, the gospels do share some similarities with the noncanonical account. In the gospels, the charges levied against Jesus include heresy, disobedience to the religious authorities, divisiveness, and claming to be the Messiah. Pilate took little interest in these accusations, asking only a cursory question of Jesus before announcing that his accusers had not presented a solid case. By instructing the Temple authorities to decide the issue themselves, Pilate was following a well-established Roman precedent of staying out of local religious disputes.

Realizing that the Roman procurator was not going to resolve the matter to their satisfaction, the Temple authorities then claimed that Jesus was traveling about Judea and Galilee stirring up the people. Pilate might not have been interested in the earlier charges against Jesus which turned on the intricacies of Jewish law and theology, but this latest accusation caught his attention: the one thing Rome demanded of all its subjects was civil obedience and domestic stability. Galilee was already a hotbed of political turmoil, and there had been clashes between Roman soldiers and the Jewish Zealot party, which sought to overthrow Roman rule. If Jesus had been involved in seditious acts, he represented a far more serious threat than Pilate had originally believed.

Upon learning that Jesus was from Galilee, Pilate ordered

that Jesus be taken to Herod Antipas to be tried. The son of Herod the Great, Herod Antipas had, upon his father's death, been given the title of Tetrarch and jurisdiction over Galilee and Peraea. But although Jesus was one of Herod's subjects, Pilate, as procurator, had ultimate authority for all of Judea, of which Jerusalem was the capital. His sending Jesus to Herod must therefore be viewed as an attempt to maneuver out of a difficult situation: concerned that there might be civil unrest if the Temple authorities did not get their way, but not seeing any basis to the Temple authorities' charges against Jesus, Pilate wanted to absolve himself of responsibility for Jesus' death.

Luke 23 indicates that Herod Antipas wanted little more than to have his sport with Jesus, to have Jesus entertain him with a miracle or great sign. After questioning Jesus, Herod allowed his soldiers to humiliate Jesus; then, claiming that he could find no justification for the charges against Jesus, Herod had him returned to Pilate.

Pilate, noting that neither he nor Herod had found Jesus guilty of any charges, declared his intention to chastise and then release Jesus, and had him sent into the Praetorium. The scourging that followed may have been one more attempt to placate the Temple authorities; it was the harshest physical punishment, short of death, Pilate could have ordered. Tying Jesus to a stone pillar, the soldiers stripped him to the waist and lashed him using a whip studded with sharp pieces of metal or stone. The Church would later interpret this punishment as the fulfillment of an ancient prophesy that the Messiah would be "bruised" for the sake of his people.

But the Temple authorities, still unsatisfied, began to incite the growing crowd outside the fortress. Pilate had no desire to make a martyr out of Jesus, but this mob was beginning to worry him. He tried one last compromise. Matthew's gospel explains that it was the custom at Passover to release any one prisoner of the people's choosing. Pilate offered the crowd the choice of Jesus or Barabbas, a well-known insurrectionist and murderer who was being held in prison. The crowd chose Barabbas, and Pilate acceded to its wish. Ordering a pitcher of water and a bowl to be brought to where he was sitting, Pilate symbolically washed his hands of the entire situation.

Back in the Praetorium, the soldiers assigned to guard Jesus, acting out of boredom mixed with malice, began taunting him. As Matthew 27 relates, they mocked his claims of kingship by dressing him in the scarlet robes of royalty. Weaving together a crown of thorns, they placed it on Jesus' head, and began to beat him with the reeds from their King's Game.

And then they led him away to be crucified.

God did not spare his own Son
but delivered him up for us all.

The gospels and the noncanonical accounts describe how some people gathered at the Antonia Fortress spoke up in defense of Jesus, while others gave in to the mob hysteria and blood-lust. At the first station, we can literally stand on the same pavement stones where the crowds stood early on the morning of that first Good Friday. What would we have done had we been there?

Our thoughts turn to what we have done when we have been in similar situations. How often have we hurried past an angry mob, fearful of our own safety, not wanting to get involved, only later to shake our heads at how no one prevented a grave injustice? Or added our own angry voice and actions to those of a hostile crowd? How often have we tried to avoid taking sides for fear of upsetting one party or the other?

The first station forces us to come to grips with the perverse way in which the world so often interprets Jesus' message of compassion and forgiveness as a threat. But it does more than that: it helps us see how we can be guilty of the same misinterpretation in our own lives. As we place ourselves in the situation of those people in first century Jerusalem—reflecting on what they did to Jesus, and what they didn't do for him—we begin to view our errors of commission and omission as things done to or not done for Jesus.

Who was responsible for condemning Jesus to death? The very stones of the pavement at the Antonia Fortress seem to remind us that we too are implicated.

The Second Station

Jesus Takes Up His Cross

One became a Roman citizen either through birth or by receiving it as an award from the government. Not only was citizenship an honor, it also carried distinct privileges. A Roman citizen could travel freely anywhere throughout the empire. Anyone who dared harm or unlawfully hinder him in his travels was severely punished to the full extent of the law—more often than not, that meant harsh corporal, if not capital, punishment. Moreover, Roman citizens who had been found guilty of a crime could, after hearing their sentence, automatically appeal it to the Emperor. Thus, when the authorities sentenced St. Paul to death, he promptly claimed his citizenship and asserted his right to state his case in person before Nero. The authorities had no recourse but to obey the law and to protect him while he was transported to Rome.

Roman citizenship, or a lack of it, also determined the

form of execution meted out to the condemned prisoner. Those who had committed serious offenses were executed by the sword; this was considered to be a swift and merciful form of death. Non-Romans were not afforded this privilege. Although there were many residents throughout Israel and the other provinces who could claim citizenship, Jesus was not among them. Over the centuries, the Romans had devised a number of different forms of execution, all of which were intentionally slow, brutal, and torturous—the better to make a public example of the criminal. Of all the forms of execution, crucifixion was considered to be the harshest.

Church art has traditionally depicted Jesus slowly and painfully dragging his cross behind him through the streets of the Old City. Although this makes for a powerful image, it is probably not accurate. After Jesus had been sentenced to death by Pilate, the Roman soldiers would have untied his hands, placed the crossbar, or horizontal piece of the cross, over his shoulders like a yoke, and tied his wrists and arms to it. The vertical portion would already have been in place at the execution site.

The purpose of tying the condemned prisoner to the cross in this fashion was twofold. First, even in the very narrow streets of the Old City, there was always the potential for escape or rescue by one's allies. Any form of diversion, from an armed confrontation to a carefully-staged accident, could have been employed to distract the soldiers from their task, thereby allowing the prisoner's friends to spirit him away to safety. The weight and width of the heavy piece of timber, along with the sheer awkwardness of carrying it, helped prevent that from happening. Second, the sight of a prisoner laboring under the weight of the crossbar as he was led to his execution served as an extremely vivid object lesson to other would-be criminals, far more powerful than words of admonition or a simple recitation of the legal code.

The second station, like the first, is found at the Antonia Fortress, but whereas the first is within the remains of the Praetorium, the second is near the Chapel of Flagellation. This very small chapel of modern design was built on the ruins and foundation of a twelfth-century oratory erected by the Crusaders. Above the altar is a stained glass window depicting Jesus being bound to the cross. Outside the chapel, preserved in an open pavilion, are the original paving stones, rough hewn so as to give traction to dray animals and pedestrians alike.

II

The Lord has laid on him the iniquity of us all; for the transgression of my people was he stricken.

At the second station, we find ourselves once again among the jeering crowds. Whether we are close to the front, so that we can see the Roman soldiers' rough treatment of the condemned prisoners, or near the rear, a safer distance away, we cannot avoid the question: what are we willing to do for Jesus' sake?

For Christians in some parts of the world, taking up one's cross and following Jesus does literally mean being willing to die for one's faith. But the vast majority of us, especially in the Western hemisphere, will live and die without ever being challenged like that. For us, the operative question should be: are we willing to *live* for Jesus? Living for Jesus means making the sometimes very difficult decision to "die" to impulses in ourselves and in society that debase human life—for example, to stand up against prejudice, injustice, and oppression. Living for Jesus also means being willing to walk alongside another person through a time of illness, trial, or intense emotional and psychological suffering. It means continuing to reach out and make ourselves vulnerable to those who, although they need help, often resist the offer and almost never express their gratitude when they do accept it.

In the Parable of the Sower, Jesus likened the seed that fell on rocky soil to those individuals who would stay with him only until things began to get rough. In his parables of the king going to war and of the man building a tower, he emphasized the importance of counting the cost before making a commitment. As we stand at the second station, we see Jesus fully committing himself by being willing to sacrifice his life for the sake of the world. This commitment would take him along the *Via Dolorosa* and eventually to Golgotha and a tomb.

What about us? Following in the way of the cross will ultimately lead us to resurrection, as it did for Jesus. But the journey will also lead us through what the British lay theologian C. S. Lewis described as the "shadowlands," times of despair and anguish when the light of the resurrection seems to have been extinguished.

Are we willing to remain true to our commitment to Jesus even in those times? Have we counted the cost?

The Third Station

Jesus Falls the First Time

Many of the details in the gospels themselves cannot be independently verified. Perhaps, therefore, the gospels should be viewed more as historical novels than as painstakingly documented biographies. At the minimum, we should never mistake them for complete and exhaustive accounts of all Jesus' deeds and sayings.

The curious mind, like nature itself, abhors a vacuum. Drawn to the gaps in the gospels' accounts of Jesus' life and ministry, the human imagination seeks to fill in the missing elements. And so the third station, the first of the six noncanonical stations, should be seen as a creative embellishment of the Passion narrative.

The gospels tell us that it was about the third hour, approximately nine o'clock in the morning, when Pilate condemned Jesus to the cross. The streets that day would have been jammed with thousands of men hurrying to the Temple to make their Passover sacrifice. What with the jostling of the crowds, the goading of the soldiers, and, of course, the weight and awkwardness of the crossbar lashed to his shoulders, it is entirely plausible that Jesus would have lost his footing.

Rather than contradict the gospel accounts, this little vignette amplifies the drama inherent in them. But pathos aside, why was it deemed significant enough to be included among the stations? The answer lies in the theological free-for-all of the Church's first centuries. Almost from the very beginning, the Church was besieged by innumerable heresies and wild interpretations about the nature and person of Jesus Christ. From the book of Acts and the earliest Pauline epistles, it is clear that Paul was not the only missionary traveling about the eastern Mediterranean spreading the Good News of Jesus Christ. We also know that the four evangelists were not the only people who wrote narratives about Jesus' life and teachings. However well intentioned these writers and itinerant preachers were, it was incumbent on the developing Church to bring some consistency to the teachings and beliefs about Jesus. This process took several hundred years; it wasn't until the fourth century that the canon of the New Testament was established in its present form.

During that time, a number of markedly different understandings of who Jesus was swirled throughout the Church. Some very sincere Christians, for instance, believed that Jesus was a fully divine entity, much like the ancient Roman and Greek gods and goddesses, whose appearance in human form was only an apparition. Others thought Jesus was fully human, but such a good and righteous man that God granted him divine status. This latter belief, known as Arianism, was extremely popular for several centuries. Indeed, for a time it seemed that it might become the official teaching of the Church. What ultimately became accepted as the orthodox position, however, was the theology now codified in the Apostles', Nicene, and Athanasian creeds—namely, that Jesus was both fully human and fully divine. True God in every respect, he nevertheless lived a completely human life, and died a painfully real death on the cross.

Real people stumble and fall all the time. By commemorating an everyday occurrence, the third station underscores the teaching that Jesus was not simply a remote deity—he became one of us and experienced all the joys and sorrows that come with the human condition.

III

Surely he has borne our griefs and carried our sorrows.

For many years the third station was marked with little more than a Roman numeral III on a nearby wall. After World War II, however, Polish soldiers who moved to Israel were granted permission to build a chapel at this site as a place for prayer and meditation. Inside, a beautifully executed sculpture by Thaddeus Zielensky depicts Jesus collapsing beneath the weight of the cross. Beneath it is an inscription from Lamentations 1:16: "The Comforter that should relieve my soul is far from me." Gazing at this sculpture, we realize that our own sins—our angry words, hateful attitudes, and vengeful or selfish behavior, as well as our acts of cowardice and the things we've left undone—have added to the weight of the cross that Jesus carries.

In our own lives, we have all experienced the heartbreak of watching a loved one fall under the weight of the world. Regardless of whether the cause is mental or physical illness, financial problems, an unjust accusation, substance abuse, loneliness, or the dashing of some cherished dream, we hurt because our loved one is hurting. But what is our response when the person who stumbles is someone we dislike, someone who has opposed our plans or thwarted our hopes? What if the person who stumbles is a self-important public official who is being unceremoniously dismissed or a business executive who is being led off to prison in handcuffs, a member of the opposite political party who is being publicly humiliated? What if it is a drunk who is being taunted by adolescents, or a mentally ill homeless person whose disturbing conversations with inanimate objects cause an uncomfortable store owner to shoo her away?

Do we have compassion for such people? Or do we get enjoyment out of seeing their humiliation or comeuppance? Often, the instinctive response is to avert our eyes, busy ourselves in our own affairs, thinking all the while, "I'm glad it's not me." But if we are truly following in Jesus' footsteps, isn't a bolder, more compassionate response possible? If we really believed that the disgraced or humiliated person was Jesus himself, how would we respond then?

IV

The Fourth Station

Jesus Meets His Mother

History seems compressed within the walls of Jerusalem's Old City, where many sites are located in close proximity. The *Via Dolorosa* is no exception. It is just a matter of a few yards to go from the third station across to the fourth, where, according to tradition, Jesus encountered his mother. A mosaic on the floor of the Church of Our Lady of the Spasm depicts two footsteps pointing to the north and west. Supposedly, this marks the exact spot where the Blessed Virgin Mary stood as she watched Jesus pass by on the way to his death.

There is no specific reference in any of the gospels to a Good Friday encounter between Jesus and Mary until he was nailed to the cross at Golgotha. Nor do the noncanonical texts mention such an earlier meeting. But no doubt the people who helped shape the stations over the centuries were very familiar with John 19:25–27, which tells of how Jesus, from the cross, spotted several of his followers in the crowd, including his mother and the disciple John (referred to in this gospel as the "disciple whom he loved"). "Woman, here is your son!" said Jesus, transferring the care of his mother to that disciple. Perhaps, in its earliest form, this station was located on Calvary instead of on the streets of Jerusalem. But given the heart-wrenching quality of the scene John describes, it is easy to understand how one might think that the creation of an additional encounter between a mother and her dying son would have been equally powerful. Moreover, there is a dramatic integrity to placing it here. Immediately following the scene in which Jesus falls for the first time, this station helps cast the human nature of Jesus in high relief. Like any other human, Jesus stumbled under the weight of a heavy burden, and also like every other human, he had a mother. The fourth station, in other words, functions as an object lesson in the early Church's struggle to combat theologies that denied Jesus' dual nature.

The creation of the fourth station also serves as a testimony to the growing importance of the cult of the Virgin in church worship. Although Mary figures prominently in the narratives of Jesus' birth, she is, for the most part a minor character in the gospels. She is mentioned in the story of Jesus' dedication at the Temple, and several other times in accounts of Jesus' ministry; she appears at the foot of the cross in John's gospel, and once more in the Acts of the Apostles. In non-canonical, Syriac-language texts from the second century, however, Mary is portrayed as the protectoress of the early Church in and around Jerusalem, a source of money and advice for that developing religious community. By the fifth century, she had come to play an important role in the liturgical life of the Eastern church, where she was given the title *Theotokos* (God-bearer). Worshippers would pray to her to intercede with Jesus on their behalf. By the sixth century, many Eastern and Western churches ascribed to the Assumption—the belief that Mary was taken up into heaven without having to undergo the decay of physical death.

Initially portrayed as an ordinary woman chosen by God, Mary came to be seen as preeminent among all the saints as an object of veneration and adoration. The fourth station serves as a partial record of that transformation.

IV

A sword will pierce your own soul also and fill your heart with bitter pain.

In a perfect world, there would be an orderly stream of one generation gently succeeding the next. Parents would never die young but would live to a ripe old age, passing from life to death in their sleep. Their children would grieve the loss and wish they had spent more time with their parents, but they would understand that death is an integral part of the human experience. In that perfect world, parents would never suffer the unspeakable pain and indignity of having to watch their child die.

But in our far-from-perfect world, parents must sometimes go through this most difficult of life's experiences. With the jeers of Jesus' enemies assaulting her ears, what jumble of emotions did Mary feel as she saw her son being led away to a violent and unjust death? This son who had always been something of a mystery to her—there were so many questions she still needed to ask him. But now it was too late.

In the words of the Church's liturgy for the Stations of the Cross, "What likeness can I use to comfort you, O virgin daughter of Zion? For vast as the sea is your ruin." As we stand at the fourth station, perhaps on the mosaic where tradition teaches that Mary stood on Good Friday, we are no longer mere spectators, safely removed from the events taking place—we now stand shoulder-to-shoulder with Mary in her moment of extreme anguish.

It is often said that a heart must be broken in order for its capacity for love to be increased. Resisting the temptation to distance ourselves from Mary's heart and suffering, we allow ourselves to feel its full devastation.

The Fifth Station

Simon of Cyrene Helps Jesus Carry the Cross

The fifth station is found along the narrow streets of the Old City, only a short distance from the fourth station. Those passing along the route can easily miss it, for unlike most of the other stations, there is no magnificent church here, nor any other building or shrine of significance. There is only an open doorway in the wall, marked with a Roman numeral V, and a stone with the Latin inscription, *Simon Cyrenae Crux Imponitor* ("here Simon of Cyrene was forced to carry the cross").

Even though Jesus had walked only a few hundred yards since leaving the Antonia Fortress, by this point he was probably exhausted physically, emotionally and spiritually. Perhaps he was moving too slowly or unsteadily to satisfy the Roman soldiers, who, sensing the mounting tensions in the crowd, wanted to complete their task and return to the safety of their barracks as quickly as possible. Then, too, the religious authorities might have been imploring the soldiers to make haste—they wanted to ensure that the bodies of the soon-to-be crucified men could be taken down and buried before sundown, when the Passover Sabbath began.

Enter Simon, one of the many minor characters in the New Testament who make brief appearances and then disappear. Both Matthew and Mark record that this man, a visitor to Jerusalem from the city of Cyrene in North Africa, was ordered by the soldiers escorting Jesus to the execution site to assist him in carrying the cross. Mark mentions the name of his children—Rufus and Alexander—but these are the only other details we are given.

Was Simon known as a follower of Jesus, and did the soldiers intentionally pick him out of the crowd as a warning to all Jesus' disciples that they would soon meet the same fate as their teacher? The more plausible scenario seems to be that he was a bystander who happened to be in the wrong place at the wrong time. He and his family had come up to Jerusalem to take their lamb to the altar at the Temple, make their sacrifice, and then celebrate the *Seder,* the traditional Passover meal. They never imagined that they would be caught up in the events of Good Friday.

And yet, when the call came to help Jesus bear his burden, Simon put aside his own plans and preferences and shouldered the load.

Whoever does not bear his own cross and come after me cannot be my disciple.

As Jesus prayed in the Garden of Gethsemane the night before he was taken prisoner, he asked God to let the cup pass from him—to find some way other than crucifixion for God's purposes to be accomplished. But when it became clear that there was no other way, Jesus reaffirmed his commitment to God's will.

Similarly, a commitment to Jesus is not simply a "spiritual" matter—it necessitates real-world obligations that we don't so much choose as have thrust upon us. Each of us, in other words, has a cross to bear. Although it is different for each of us, Jesus' message is the same: "If any want to become my followers," he told his disciples, "let them deny themselves, take up their cross and follow me."

Jesus has no one but us to help him bear the burdens of

the world. Are we willing to alter our own plans for our lives in order to answer his call? Simon, about whom so little is known, functions here in the fifth station as a universal type—an example of the kind of openness Jesus asks of us. In his willingness to bear the burdens that come with a life lived in communion with Jesus—no matter how inconvenient, unexpected, and onerous the burdens—Simon serves as an icon of faithful discipleship.

The Sixth Station

Veronica Wipes the Face of Jesus

Even if one wishes to discount the story of a woman named Veronica who stood at this site to wipe the brow of Jesus, the stories associated with her, and the saga of her miraculous cloth, we cannot. This Station makes it clear that Jesus—the True Face—was present at this spot as he carried his cross toward Calvary.

Although less than a hundred yards from the fifth station and only a few steps from the seventh, the sixth station is still easy to miss. The only indications of its existence are the Roman numeral VI and the stylized word "Station" on a wooden door that leads into an Armenian Christian church and, near the door, also in stylized letters, the name "Veronica."

The event commemorated involved a brave woman named Veronica, who, according to an eighth-century legend, defied the Roman soldiers, went up to Jesus as he was passing by and wiped his bloody brow with a small cloth or handkerchief. Much like the Shroud of Turin, the cloth miraculously maintained Jesus' impression or likeness on it.

Just who was this woman? Although there is no biblical mention of the wiping of Jesus' brow, the noncanonical *Acts of Pilate* does refer to a Veronica (the name is the Latinized version of the Coptic "Beronice") who was one of the people who testified before Pilate about Jesus' miracles and good deeds. Before she began her testimony, the text relates, the Temple authorities tried to prevent her from speaking, claiming that it was a violation of their law for a woman to speak openly and freely before men or to give a legal statement. Pilate, already irritated that the authorities were troubling him with what seemed like a petty matter, allowed her to speak. Veronica told the procurator that she had suffered for twelve years from an "issue of blood" and that Jesus' touch had healed her. This part of the story has led some scholars to suggest that Veronica may have been the anonymous woman mentioned in Matthew 9:21, who was cured of the same condition by touching the hem of Jesus' robe.

According to another legend, the emperor Tiberius, suffering from a grave physical ailment, learned of a wonderful miracle worker and healer in Jerusalem by the name of Jesus. He dispatched a trusted officer, Volusianus, to Pilate, with orders for the procurator to send this "physician" to Rome. By this time, however, Jesus' crucifixion, resurrection, and ascension had already occurred. Pilate, worried that the emperor would be angry with him because of his part in Jesus' execution, tried to stall Volusianus: he sent him away for fourteen days, claiming that he would search for Jesus in the meantime. On his way back to the inn where he was staying, Volusianus had a chance encounter with Veronica on the street and asked her if she knew anything about Jesus. She told him the Passion story, adding that she still had the cloth that bore the likeness of the Lord's face, and that it had miraculous powers to cure all those who were ill. Volusianus offered to buy the cloth; Veronica refused to sell it, but did agree to lend it to him so that he could take it to Rome. (The relic that has been kept at St. Peter's Church in Rome since 1297 is said to be this very same cloth.)

More interesting than the legends themselves is the way the fourth station makes use of them for instructional purposes. Note how this station strikes a different thematic and theological chord. The third, fourth, and fifth stations all underscore Jesus' humanity. Here, it is the healing power of Jesus' divinity that is highlighted. According to some popular heresies of the early centuries, Jesus did not actually die on the cross; a substitute died in his place. Jesus was allowed to escape and left the public scene. Such beliefs are flatly contradicted here. Just as the medieval historian Giraldus Cambrensis suggested "true face" or "true image" as the etymology of the name Veronica, the sixth station makes the point that the Jesus who suffered and died on the cross in Jerusalem and the God of the Universe are one and the same. The man whose brow Veronica wiped was the true image of God.

Note also how the event memorialized here turns the social mores of the time upside down. Back then, men had nothing to do with women who were not members of their immediate family—yet Jesus healed a woman he didn't know in public. And although women in that society were also prohibited from having contact with men outside their immediate family, Veronica, emboldened by Jesus' act of compassion, reached out to him in his hour of suffering.

VI

Restore us, O Lord God of hosts; show the light of your countenance, and we shall be saved.

Whom do we seek? No myth or legend, nor even a great man. The Jesus we seek and serve is the fountainhead of all life, the Word made flesh. Here at the sixth station, we are invited to acknowledge this reality and to confess, as Peter did in Matthew's gospel, "You are the Messiah, the Son of the living God."

Cosmic implications of salvation history are here juxtaposed with simple acts of compassion. Touched by the saving love of Jesus, we begin to discern ways in which we can be of service to him. That love also makes us bold, gives us the strength to persevere through scorn, deprivation, and even danger in following Jesus. Others saw Jesus suffering and let him pass by. Veronica did what she could, where she could, with what she had. When we reach out to others in compassion we too are wiping Jesus' brow.

The Seventh Station

Jesus Falls a Second Time

Moving from the sixth to the seventh station, the *Via Dolorosa* goes up a very slight, gradual incline. It is easy not to notice this rise, but for a condemned man carrying his cross, even it would have been agony. An ancient Roman column with the numeral VII marks the spot where, according to tradition, Jesus fell a second time. Throughout their empire, on columns nearest the city gate through which prisoners were taken for execution, the Romans published the names of those who had been condemned. So why is there no city gate near this column? The answer lies in a sixteenth-century architectural blunder.

There have been numerous changes to the original walls of Jerusalem's Old City over the past three millennia. When David conquered the Jebusite city of Jerusalem around 1000 BCE, he claimed Mount Zion as his own. He and his successors expanded this private fiefdom, which became known as the City of David, and had walls built around it. Torn down when the Babylonians captured Jerusalem in 587 BCE, the walls were rebuilt under the direction of Nehemiah seventy years later, when the Jewish exiles returned from captivity. This pattern of destruction and rebuilding repeated itself intermittently over the following two thousand years as the Romans, Persians, Crusaders, and Muslims all laid siege to the city. In the sixteenth century, the walls as we know them today were rebuilt under the direction of the Ottoman Sultan Suleiman the Great. Suleiman wanted to have the ramparts restored exactly as they stood in King David's time, but instead of including Mount Zion—the City of David—within the walls, his architects incorporated the opposite end of the city. The end result is that it is a far greater distance to the site of the crucifixion today than it was on that first Good Friday.

VII

But as for me, I am a worm and no man, scorned by all and despised by the people.

According to the ancient traditions instituted on the first Passover (immediately prior to the Exodus) each Jewish family or group of approximately ten adults would take a pure, unblemished male lamb, ritually sacrifice it, and then eat it according to the instructions given to Moses. For many centuries, this ritual was performed in people's homes and in the villages throughout the country. But after the construction of the Temple during the reign of King Solomon, and then later, after the Second Temple had been built following the Babylonian Exile, people seemed to have developed a strong preference for observing this holy day in Jerusalem. Even today, many Jewish families exclaim, "Next year in Jerusalem" at the conclusion of the Passover meal as an expression of the hope that the coming year will find them near Jerusalem's Western Wall at Passover.

At the very time that these annual sacrifices for sins were taking place, Jesus was making his way toward Calvary. The symbolic significance of these two events occurring at the same time was not lost on the Church. John 1:29 quotes John the Baptist as saying, "Here is the Lamb of God, who takes away the sin of the world," upon first meeting Jesus. Thus, Passover became the lens through which early Christians interpreted Jesus' crucifixion: just as the Passover had been the means of liberating the children Israel from their bondage in Egypt, Jesus' death was the means of liberating the whole world from the bondage of sin.

Jesus—God's only son, the one pure, unblemished, sinless individual in the history of the world—willingly became a sacrificial lamb for our sake. For us, he allowed himself to be falsely accused, brutally tortured, and unjustly sentenced. It was not just the weight of the cross he carried that caused his knees to buckle—he was also bearing the weight of the sins of the whole world on his shoulders.

And yet he remained faithful to the vision he had for us all, a vision of life lived in intimate connection with God. Behold the Lamb of God.

The Eighth Station

Jesus Meets the Women of Jerusalem

This station, marked by the Greek word *Nika* ("victor") carved into a stone wall, memorializes an event recorded in Luke 23:27–28. Pausing to console a group of grieving women who are following the procession to the execution site, Jesus says to them, "Daughters of Jerusalem, do not weep for me, but weep for yourselves and for your children."

The gospels relate numerous stories of how Jesus contravened the norms and religious codes of his culture. He performed healings on the Sabbath. He did not ritually wash his hands before eating. And whereas the Pharisees and others went out of their way in an attempt to avoid social outcasts such as tax collectors and the mentally ill, Jesus embraced them.

Similarly, he often broke the rules that helped maintain the subjugation of women. Indeed, he was far more egalitarian in his treatment of women than the prevailing standards of the time. The gospels indicate not only that a number of women accompanied him and his disciples, but that they were considered important members of this larger circle of disciples. By stopping to show concern for these women of Jerusalem, whom he may not have even known, Jesus went against the norm that forbade men and women who didn't know one another from associating freely. It wasn't that he lacked respect for social convention. It was simply that when confronted with a norm, tradition, even institution that hindered rather than promoted the dignified treatment of people as full human beings, his response was always clear and unhesitating.

But what to make of his advice to the women—"weep for yourselves and for your children"? Several times in the gospels, Jesus refers to tribulations that would befall his people. Was he foretelling the First Jewish Revolt, which occurred only a few decades after his death? Many of the women in the crowd on that first Good Friday would see their husbands, fathers, brothers, and sons die in that war. Or was he warning his followers of the persecutions to come at the hands of the Romans? We can only speculate.

VIII

Those who sowed with tears will reap with songs of joy.

Is a concern for the welfare of others, especially people who make us feel uncomfortable or to whom we have little connection, something we demonstrate only when it is convenient—when we have the time and the emotional energy? Jesus drew everyone into his circle of compassion: the righteous and the wicked, the wealthy and the destitute, those who controlled the corridors of power and those who were excluded.

Pain and distress have a way of narrowing our field of vision; our sphere of awareness and concern collapses around whatever it is that is causing us to suffer. But at the height of his physical, emotional, and spiritual torment, Jesus managed not just to notice but to respond to the suffering of others. And not only the suffering of important people, but the distress of those who went largely unnoticed in the society of his time.

What enabled Jesus to set aside his own distress to care for these grieving women of Jerusalem? How can we learn to carve out space in our preoccupied minds and busy lives to make room for the concerns of others? Perhaps Jesus' message to the women of Jerusalem—"do not weep for me, but weep for yourselves and for your children"—offers a clue.

To be sure, self-denial plays an important role in Christian discipleship, but when it comes to giving ourselves freely to the service of others, it is the extension of the boundaries of the self rather than the denial of the self that enables this to happen. By including others in the definition of our own self-interest, we are able to see and respond to their needs much more readily. Their loss hurts us just as much as if it had happened to us, for in a very real sense, it has.

Jesus was able to show compassion so spontaneously and fearlessly because he felt no separation between himself and others. Even as his body was being tortured and his life was being taken away, he showed us what the Body of Christ was all about.

The Ninth Station

Jesus Falls a Third Time

The noncanonical ninth station is the first stop along the *Via Dolorosa* where there is tangible evidence of the Crusaders' presence in Jerusalem, which lasted nearly a hundred years. After capturing the city in 1099, the Crusaders made like they intended to stay, erecting chapels, oratories, shrines, as well as numerous secular buildings. In the process, they destroyed many ancient Jewish and Roman buildings. They also intentionally damaged or profaned buildings sacred to Islam—most notably, the Mosque of the Dome of the Rock, Islam's third holiest site, which the Crusaders converted to their own use.

Entering through the doorway to the right of the column that marks the ninth station, one sees the evidence of Christianity's continuity down through the ages. Just beyond the doorway are the remains of the courtyard that once served as the refectory for the Crusader Canons of the Church of the

Holy Sepulchre. (The Crusader canons were men in holy orders who were also Knights Templar, one of the two principal military orders of medieval Christendom. They were thus soldiers and teachers of church law.) Although the refectory's ceiling has long since collapsed, the walls, arches, and columns remain. Within the courtyard are the vividly painted doors to the hermitages where Ethiopian Coptic monks and nuns have resided for centuries. And not far from these cells, a small, dark stairway leads down into an ancient Coptic chapel.

Then there is the Church of the Holy Sepulchre itself, which dates back to the fourth century. One of the most important shrines in all of Christendom, it has been rebuilt and remodeled many times over the years; the Crusaders' addition of a refectory and barracks being just one phase. Beneath a wing of the Church of the Holy Sepulchre is the Chapel of St. Helena. In that chapel lies one of most cherished relics in Christendom.

Shortly after her conversion, Helena, the mother of the emperor Constantine, made a pilgrimage to the Holy Land to worship at the places connected with the life of Jesus and to find relics associated with him and the early Christian saints. According to legend, on the site where the present chapel stands, she was presented with the last remaining piece of the cross on which Jesus had been crucified, a section of wood about three feet in length. The cross had been carefully preserved, along with the crown of thorns and the spear which the Roman soldier had pierced his side (the crown and spear have since been lost or destroyed). Helena had the section of the cross cut into three pieces. Two of the pieces (now lost) she sent to other important Christian shrines outside of Jerusalem. The third piece, a fragment about ten inches long, lies in the Chapel of St. Helena under heavy guard in what is known as the Crypt of the Invention, or the Crypt of the Finding of the Cross.

He was led like a lamb to the slaughter;
and like a sheep that before its shearers is mute,
so he opened not his mouth.

In the centuries that followed Jesus' crucifixion, the cross would be seen as a symbol of our victory over sin and death. People would venerate even small shards that had supposedly come from the cross on which Jesus was crucified, attributing miraculous healing powers to them. But on that Friday some two thousand years ago, a cross conjured up images not of liberation but of brutal torture, not of triumph, but of shame, scandal, and failure.

Jesus could see Golgotha (literally, the "place of the skull"), the hill just outside the city where his execution would take place, coming into view. A crowd was gathering to witness the event. The worst was still to come. He knew that death would not be quick. This was not the way he had hoped it would end, but the cup could not be removed from him.

The heavy wooden crossbar dug into his bleeding shoulders and back. A shudder passed through his exhausted body, and he stumbled yet again.

"Abba, Father, not what I will..."

X

The Tenth Station

Jesus is Stripped of His Garments

Through the main entrance to the Church of the Holy Sepulchre and in a chamber just off to the right, there is a flight of stairs that leads to what church tradition identifies as the site of Jesus' crucifixion. Given that the tenth station is located inside the church, at the top of the stairs in the Chapel of the Divestiture, it can be difficult to imagine how this was where Mount Calvary stood. But it must be remembered that when the Church of the Holy Sepulchre built, the stone was cleared down to the bedrock before the foundation was laid.

Artistic depictions of the crucifixion almost always show Jesus with a cloth wrapped around his waist, much like a Roman toga. But in keeping with the Romans' reason for staging public crucifixions, which was to deter crime, the custom was to strip the condemned prisoner naked. This form of humiliation intensified the psychological devastation of the experience. Indeed, the image of their Lord and Savior being shamed in this way proved so shocking to the imagination of early Christians that the apocryphal *Acts of Pilate* relates that after the soldiers stripped Jesus of his garments, "they girt his loins with a cloth of linen." Moreover, it sometimes took days for the person being crucified to die; exposing his flesh to the scorching sun and winds of summer or the freezing rain and occasional snows of winter would only intensify the physical agony.

Back then, a person was identified by his clothing far more than is the case today. From the emperor in his purple robes, to senators in their white togas, to the newest recruit in the Roman legions, down to the lowliest slave, everyone had a uniform or customary manner of dress that served to place him within the social hierarchy. So when he was stripped naked, not only was Jesus shamed in front of friend and foe alike, he was also symbolically divested of his power and authority. The sign that Pontius Pilate had nailed to the cross—here is Jesus, King of the Jews, it proclaimed in Greek, Latin, and Hebrew—merely reinforced the mockery.

X

They gave me gall to eat, and when I was thirsty they gave me vinegar to drink.

Never let your weaknesses be exposed. Use cunning and guile to maintain your advantage. Make use of the symbols of authority to silence the voices of those who disagree with you. Employ fear, even force if necessary, to bring your opponents around to your way of thinking. These are the lessons of power. This is the way to get on in the world.

But it was not the way of Jesus. Although it was well within his power to call down legions of angels to rescue him and destroy his enemies, he did not. He had come to introduce another way of being into the world—one that relied on justice, mercy, and the equitable treatment of all instead of on compulsion.

The very logic of Jesus' way meant that he couldn't force it on people; they had to choose it of their own free will. In order to transform the world, he had to put himself at the mercy of the world. And so for the sake of this way of being, Jesus emptied himself on the cross, surrendering everything from his divinity to the last vestiges of his human dignity.

The Eleventh Station

Jesus is Nailed to the Cross

The three holes carved into the rock at the eleventh station are supposed to be where the crosses on that first Good Friday were driven into the ground. As implausible as this claim is, it is not unusual for pilgrims to pray before the open altar that is situated over these holes, kneel down and kiss the site, and then light a votive candle and place it in the sand-filled tray nearby.

Sculptures or paintings depicting the crucifixion often show Jesus with his arms stretched out on the front of the horizontal beam of the cross and his hands nailed to the wood. But driving nails through the soft flesh of the palms and into the front of the cross would have enabled the prisoner to fall off or even pull himself loose (although with much pain and difficulty). Therefore, the nails were typically driven into the bone of the lower arm, near the wrist. Given that iron nails were expensive when they were able to be had at all, the criminal's outstretched arms were often bound with strong ropes to the horizontal bar of the cross, making escape impossible. In Jesus' case, the gospel accounts of his appearances after his resurrection indicate that he had nail holes in his hands. For that to have been the case, the soldiers would have had to bend his arms over the top of the horizontal beam and nail his hands to the top or back of the crossbar.

After a prisoner's arms had been secured, his feet were either lashed or nailed to a small platform farther down the vertical beam of the cross. Depictions of the crucifixion often show Jesus standing upright, straight-legged, or even suspended by his hands. But the Romans usually put this platform high enough so that the condemned man had to bend his knees, thereby making it all but impossible for him to get a good footing, and increasing his agony all the more.

The fastening of the criminal to the cross was done on the ground. Ropes and wooden struts were then used to pull the cross upright and drop it into place in a hole carved into the rock. The sudden jarring as the cross fell into position often sent the condemned man into shock. When the victim's chest and arm muscles could no longer support the weight of his entire body, he would slump down. Eventually, he would drown, as his chest cavity filled with fluid.

The gospels interpret Jesus' crucifixion between two common criminals as the fulfillment of an Old Testament prophecy that the Messiah would be listed among the sinners. (Although these two criminals are not mentioned by name in any of the gospels, *The Acts of Pilate* identifies them as Dymas and Gestas.) These circumstances lent credence to subsequent accusations that Jesus was himself a criminal and an insurrectionist. Indeed, one of the later charges against Christians was that their worship of a criminal constituted an act of rebellion against the emperor.

They pierce my hands and my feet; they stare and gloat over me.

When Abraham was preparing to sacrifice his only son, a ram appeared in the thicket nearby. God had spared Isaac by providing a substitute.

But here at Golgotha, when it was God's son who was about to be sacrificed, there would be no ram in the thicket.

The Twelfth Station

Jesus Dies on the Cross

An ornate Byzantine altar and magnificent icons situated directly over the bedrock of Mount Calvary highlight this station. When this site was being cleared in preparation for the laying of the foundation of the Church of the Holy Sepulchre, a split in the rock was exposed. According to church lore, this split occurred when an earthquake shook the region at the instant of Jesus' death. Alluding to an even more ancient Jewish tradition, which holds that the tomb of Adam lies beneath this site, the church legend goes on to suggest that Jesus' blood dripped through the fissure in the rock to Adam's tomb. In symbolic terms, the saving blood of Jesus Christ reached all the way back to humankind's first sinner.

The gospels and the noncanonical literature agree that Jesus died on the Day of Preparation before Passover, which that year fell on the Sabbath (Saturday), making it the ultimate high holy day. On what we now call Good Friday, Jewish men would have been patiently awaiting their turn to make their sacrifice at the Temple, then returning to their homes or wherever they were staying to roast their lamb and celebrate the Passover meal. By late afternoon, all work would have come to an end.

Two extraordinary events occurred on that day, the gospels tell us. First, a great darkness descended over the land during the three hours that Jesus hung on the cross. *The Acts of Pilate* says that after a centurion returned to Pilate to inform him that Jesus was dead, Pilate asked some of the Jews (perhaps some of the Temple authorities?) about the unusual darkness. They brushed it off, saying that it was nothing more than an eclipse. The Christian gloss on this event, however, was that heaven and earth—indeed, the entire universe—mourned Jesus' sacrificial death.

Second, the veil in the Temple—the beautiful cloth drape that covered the entrance into the holy of holies at the very center of the Temple, separating it from the rest of the building—was torn in two. The Jews firmly believed that the holy of holies was where God lived when visiting the earth. This altar and the chamber that enclosed it were so sacred that only the chief priest could enter it, and then only one day a year when, at the conclusion of all the other Passover sacrifices, he made a sacrifice on behalf of the entire nation of Israel. A rope was always tied around one of the chief priest's ankles when he entered the holy of holies, so that if he should die while in the presence of God (a very strong possibility, the people believed), his body could be dragged out.

Throughout his ministry, Jesus emphasized that God's love for humanity was not just a general love for a race or nation, but an intimate, personal love. God knows when a sparrow falls from the sky, Jesus told his followers. God has numbered the hairs on our head. Similarly, Jesus taught his disciples that they didn't need to use stiff, formal titles when praying to God. The tender, familiar names that characterize a heartfelt, rambling conversation between a father and child would do just fine. Christians interpreted the rending of the Temple veil as the confirmation of this new relationship with God that Jesus talked about. God was no longer remote, shut off from humanity. In Jesus, God had been brought near, and through Jesus, people could have immediate access to God.

XII

Christ for us became obedient unto death, even death on a cross.

Anger, grief, bewilderment, bitterness, fear for their own safety—Jesus' disciples must have felt these things and a jumble of other emotions as the sun set that day. This man who could make their hearts burn when he talked about the Scriptures—how could they carry on the work now that he was dead? Did it even make sense to continue the work? Who would follow his teachings, who would believe he was the true Son of God once they learned that he had died on the cross? Had Jesus' talk of the reign of God been a grand deception?

Interpreting the crucifixion as we do, in the light of the resurrection, it is easy for us to minimize the utter despair the disciples must have felt on Good Friday. To them, Jesus' death seemed like the end of everything, the negation of all he had said and done. As we pause at the twelfth station, we would do well to suspend what we know about Easter and let the reality of our Lord's death crash in upon us.

Our faith in the power of the resurrection is tenuous

indeed if we cannot acknowledge that on this day, the love of God was quenched.

The Thirteenth Station

The Body of Jesus is Placed in the Arms of His Mother

The thirteenth station is the first thing a pilgrim notices upon entering the Church of the Holy Sepulchre. It is located at the Stone of the Unction, a marble slab, with three candles at the head and three at the foot, that lies beneath a row of hanging lanterns. According to tradition, it was on this spot that Mary received the body of her son Jesus, and where the initial preparations for burial were made.

There is, however, no direct biblical reference to Mary's receiving Jesus' body and cradling it in her arms, as is depicted in so much religious art. John's gospel reports only that Mary, her sister, Mary Magdalene, and John (the beloved disciple) witnessed the crucifixion at Golgotha, and that Jesus, seeing his mother, transferred responsibility for her care to John. But this station, the last of the six noncanonical sites along the *Via Dolorosa,* continues the pattern established by its five predecessors. Taking the gospel narratives as their touchstone, the noncanonical stations create dramatic scenes that give the pilgrim additional access points into the story—further opportunities to connect emotionally with the events of Good Friday. The third, seventh, and ninth stations, which dramatize the times that Jesus fell while carrying his cross, underscore the physical realities of the situation, especially the weight of the cross and the genuine pain experienced. The fourth, sixth, and thirteenth stations describe encounters with women—two with Mary and one with Veronica—in which pathos and tenderness are the dominant themes. The thirteenth station is particularly poignant in this regard, masterfully juxtaposing Mary's maternal care with the savagely brutal act that has just been committed against her son.

The Stone of Unction is not authentic. In all likelihood, Jesus' body was placed on the ground after it was taken down from the cross. John's gospel tells us that Nicodemus, an influential and wealthy man who was also a secret follower of Jesus, went to Golgotha, bringing with him a large quantity of myrrh and aloes to use in preparing Jesus' body for burial. A burial shroud would have been spread out over the ground and an initial layer of spices would have been sprinkled on it. Next, the body would have been placed on the linen shroud and the remaining spices would have been poured on top. Once this was done, the shroud would have been tightly wrapped, making the body ready for burial. Luke's gospel tells us that because sunset was fast approaching and the Passover Sabbath would soon be upon them, the people preparing Jesus' body were unable to finish their work. They went home to prepare the spices and ointment, planning to return two days later to the tomb where Jesus' body had been laid, after the Sabbath observance was over.

As for finding a tomb in which to bury Jesus and securing Pilate's permission to have the body handed over, these arrangements were handled by a man named Joseph from the Judean town of Arimathea, the gospels tell us. Why Joseph? The disciples, all from the notoriously rebellious province of Galilee, were probably too closely associated with Jesus to have safely approached the procurator. Moreover, it is doubtful that they had the social standing to serve as petitioners on such a delicate mission. Nor is it likely, given the prevailing cultural norms, that Jesus' mother Mary or any of the women associated with Jesus would have been granted an audience with Pilate.

By contrast, the biblical accounts suggest that Joseph

was a wealthy and highly respected man, someone to whom Pilate would have readily granted an audience. Luke tells us that he was "a member of the council [the Sanhedrin], had not agreed to their plan and action... and he was waiting expectantly for the kingdom of God." The implication is that Joseph, like Nicodemus, was a secret disciple of Jesus who dared not reveal his true loyalty publicly. According to one non-canonical text, Joseph was Jesus' uncle and also a high-ranking official in Pilate's administration—something akin to an ombudsman or diplomatic liaison to the Sanhedrin.

Her tears run down her cheeks, and she had none to comfort her.

There is nothing as tender and as strong as a mother's love. And there is nothing as terrifying to a mother as being unable to protect her child from harm. No horror movie could be more disturbing than the image presented at the thirteenth station. Here we get a searing glimpse of what it is like when what is most precious to us in life is ripped away.

What comfort can there be in the wake of such a devastation? What balm can soothe such a loss? The world is sapped of all sense and color, all sweetness and music. Echoing the prophet Jeremiah's lament, the heart begins to question its fundamental belief in a benevolent God:

> *grief is upon me,*
> *my heart is sick.*
> *Hark, the cry of my poor people*
> *from far and wide in the land:*
> *Is the Lord not in Zion?*
> *Is her King not in her?*

The Fourteenth Station

Jesus is Laid in the Tomb

The fourteenth station, Jesus' tomb, is located in the center of the Church of the Holy Sepulchre, underneath its huge Byzantine dome. A temple to Venus, built by the Emperor Hadrian, originally occupied this site. It gave way to a Christian church that was built sometime before 135 CE. Then, in the fourth century, St. Helena had the first basilica of the Church of the Holy Sepulchre erected.

Originally, the tomb would have been outside the walls of Jerusalem, in the private garden of Joseph of Arimathea. Back then, instead of using community cemeteries or burial grounds, wealthy families tended to have private tombs carved into a rock wall on their property. Using iron tools, workers would carve a small opening into the wall and fashion a double burial chamber inside. The body would be placed on a stone shelf or ledge in the outer chamber once it had been prepared for burial. Preparations included applying sweet-smelling ointments, oils, and spices to the body to mask the odor caused by decomposition, then tightly wrapping it in a linen shroud. Much later, after the soft tissue had decomposed and the body fluids had drained away, the shrouded skeleton would be moved into the inner chamber. Several generations might eventually be buried together in this inner chamber. To seal the tomb, workmen would carve a large wheel out of solid rock, usually limestone, and place it on a track in front of the entrance. After each burial, the stone would be rolled into place and sealed with wax or pitch.

Jesus' tomb is properly referred to as the *Anastasis* or the Chapel of the Resurrection. At its heart is the two-chambered Tomb of the Redeemer. The outer chamber is known as the Chapel of the Angel, in commemoration of the angels that John's gospel describes as being present when Mary and the other women came to the tomb on Easter morning. The inner chamber, greatly remodeled in the nineteenth century, is where Jesus' body is said to have been laid, even though the custom was to place a recently prepared body on the shelf in the outer chamber.

Because of the tomb's small size and close quarters,

only a few people can enter it at a time. Visitors must often stand in long lines as they wait their turn. Many purchase a small bundle of tapers from one of the nearby kiosks, light the wicks, and then quickly extinguish them before entering the shrine.

Opposite the tomb itself, under a large rotunda built by the Crusaders, is a beautiful chapel known as the *Catholicon,* which many Christians claim is the center of the world. Only a few steps away from the rotunda is the Altar of St. Mary Magdalene, located at the site where, according to tradition, Mary stood weeping when she saw the risen Jesus for the first time. Also nearby is the Chapel of the Apparition of Jesus to his Mother where, church tradition holds, Jesus first appeared to the Blessed Virgin Mary on Easter morning.

You will not abandon me to the grave,
nor let your Holy One see corruption.

Was death the final end for Jesus? Standing in the long line to enter into Jesus' tomb, we ask the same question that generations of people have posed since that first

Easter. Our interest is not simply academic or historical: we are also wondering about the trajectory of our own lives. What, if anything, comes after death?

We can readily accept that Jesus was arrested, tried and falsely convicted, crucified, and that his body was placed in the tomb. But can our rational minds really accept that he rose from the dead? Maybe he didn't really die on the cross, we think, as pilgrims in line ahead of us enter the tomb for a few moments of prayer and meditation. Maybe he just lost consciousness on the cross; then, after he had been taken down and left in the cool tomb, he resuscitated, and rolled the stone away himself. Perhaps his disciples took his body from the tomb to give the appearance that he had indeed risen from the dead, as he had promised. That way, Jesus' teachings would have continued to be credible, and his disciples would have been able to continue his work more easily. Another possibility: maybe Pilate or the Temple authorities coerced Joseph of Arimathea into removing the body from the tomb so that it couldn't become a shrine to a martyred political opponent.

The line moves slowly forward. We look around the rotunda in the Church of the Holy Sepulchre. It seems too big and gaudy. Tourists' cameras flash constantly. And all those kiosks and stalls—so much for our Lord's attempt to make his father's house a house a prayer. Has the Church become such an institution that it has forgotten the Galilean's teachings?

We hear raised voices and follow the sounds to the main doorway. Two monks from different religious orders, one with a broom to sweep the steps, another with a smoking thurible full of sweet incense, are arguing in a language we don't understand.

Finally, we reach the entrance to the tomb. Despite our skepticism about so many of the historical claims we've heard along the pilgrim route, a sense of eagerness overtakes us. Wouldn't this have been about where the soldiers guarding the tomb stood? And is that the spot where Mary Magdalene stood weeping when she saw that the stone had been rolled away? Did the disciples pause before going inside the tomb, afraid of what they might see, and perhaps even more terrified of what they might not find there?

We have to bend down to get through the opening. We look down at the stone shelf in the outer tomb, then squeeze through the narrow entrance into the inner chamber. Our mind captures everything: the marble, the icons, the candles.

XIV

We try to imagine the scene some two thousand years ago: Joseph of Arimathea, Nicodemus, and the others would have carried Jesus' lifeless body to this exact spot and reverently laid it here, on the stone ledge. From this very spot, he rose from the dead on that first Easter morning.

After a moment's silent reflection, it is time to leave. Still crouching down, we hesitate before leaving and look back into the tomb once more—then turn to step out, and stand up straight once more. (Did Jesus do the same thing on the morning of his resurrection?) Silently, we make our way out of the Church of the Holy Sepulchre. The two monks are still arguing in the doorway as we walk back into the blazing sunlight.

We began our pilgrimage along the *Via Dolorosa* in a spirit of inquiry more than devotion. We wanted to see the places where the events of salvation history are supposed to have taken place and then make up our minds about how much of it to believe. But by the end of the pilgrimage, we realize that absolute certainty is a chimera. The tools of historical inquiry can never fully grasp a supernatural event. Although we leave the tomb from which Jesus rose from the dead, we understand that this belief must be based on faith, not empirical evidence.

Besides, whether a particular event occurred in the exact

place or even in the precise manner claimed seems less important now than the power of Jesus' life and teachings to transform individuals and communities. Jesus' message—justice, peace, compassion, forgiveness, and an abiding concern for the poor, the outcast, and the desperate among us—has been profoundly altering people's lives for nearly two thousand years, as have the stories of people whose lives have been changed by Jesus' message.

We leave now with a sense of gratitude for our fellow pilgrims along the way. By opening our hearts to the suffering Jesus endured for our sake, the *Via Dolorosa* has also opened our eyes to the evidence of Jesus' redeeming love in the people around us. And maybe that is all the proof of the resurrection we need.